EMANUELE M. BARBONI DALLA COSTA

Principles of Emotional Intelligence

Contents

The Author   v

1   Introduction   1

2   A "terrified chimpanzee"   2

3   Primary emotions   4

Anger   4

Fear   5

Sadness and Joy   6

Surprise, Contempt and Disgust   6

4   Recognizing emotions   8

5   Secondary emotions   11

Cheerfulness and Envy   12

Shame   13

Anxiety   14

Resignation   15

Jealousy   16

Hope   17

Forgiveness   18

The Offense   19

Nostalgia   20

Remorse   20

Disappointment   21

6   Where do we feel our emotions?   23

7   Towards self-realization   30

8   Conclusions   34

Training and Coaching   36

My Books   36

The Author

My name is Emanuele Barboni Dalla Costa (Milan, 1981) and I am a professional trainer of Effective and Emotional Communication, Storytelling and Creative Writing.

I live in Milan in the company of a very adorable Persian cat: Cleopatra. My goal is to help clients and students transform the way they communicate in the world.

Since 2009 I've been regularly teaching classroom and online courses dedicated to effective communication, creative writing and storytelling.

Focusing on communication for me means improving the dialogue we have with ourselves and others.

In my career, I've helped over 1,000 students in the classroom and over 5,000 online (through my video courses) to communicate better in business, relationships, and dialogue with the world.

You can get more information at https://www.emozionare.net and in the last chapter of this book (where you'll also find a little surprise reserved for you).

I wish you a good reading!

Emanuele

1

Introduction

The objective of this book is to make you know (and recognize) the primary emotions and secondary emotions to get a better understanding of yourself and, consequently, go to improve your communication.

I am a trainer and I deal with emotional communication, relational storytelling and creativity.

I have been behind the desk since 2009.

Year after year I specialized in emotional communication, which means going to arouse emotions in the other person and then receive emotions.

We know very well that the moment we go to improve our communication and go to perfect it we will get better relationships. And when relationships improve, so do many aspects of our lives.

So, having an eye towards emotions can mean a complete improvement of our daily life and the quality of our existence.

2

A "terrified chimpanzee"

There are seven primary (basic) emotions and they are those emotions that are found in any population.

They are universal emotions.

But where do our emotions come from?

Let's get into the perspective of thinking that we are "evolved chimpanzees" and we cannot get away from reasoning about the context in which this primal went.

A dangerous situation in which the goal was to survive.

This can partially explain the concept that emotions of sadness, fear or otherwise negative are present in greater numbers than positive ones, such as joy and surprise.

Our DNA is predisposed more for primary negative emotions than for positive ones and we can reason that communicating is something very difficult.

In fact, we are programmed for distrust, especially in the first moments, minutes or days.

By communicating we have to go and break through what is a wall of distrust, because we are naturally predisposed to protect our lives, like the chimpanzees mentioned earlier.

Clearly, society has appeased our primary instincts, but in a part of us there is still that "terrified chimpanzee", wary and inclined to defend its territory.

3

Primary emotions

Anger

At the first place of this list of emotions we put anger.

This is an emotion generated by frustration and is manifested through aggression, which is a characteristic that distinguishes us as human beings.

In power we are aggressive beings because we derive from a context of danger and distrust.

When we feel anger, our body stiffens and tends to vent this inner feeling through outward acts. When there were no rules and there was no society or culture, but there was only "nature", anger was vented very trivially with murder.

Even today, in some indigenous peoples there is this way to vent anger, as well as among animals.

In fact, normally in a dangerous situation there are two ways of escape: flee or attack. In the case of humans, we forcefully wear the hat of society, culture and religion that prevents us from doing so.

Anger also manifests itself very explicitly from a physical point of view, for example you clench your fists and stiffen your neck.

Fear

In second place we can put an equally important emotion as that of fear.

Fear saves us: if we were not afraid and were reckless our species would have been in danger from the beginning.

Fear is an emotion dominated by instinct that has as its goal the survival of the subject in a dangerous situation.

This feeling is a signal from our body that serves to self-protect the survival of our species. We feel fear when there is a danger, which can be real or imagined (in the latter case, fear turns into anxiety).

In fact, anxiety is a projection dictated by our previous experience of a danger in power, that is, that could happen, so our body stiffens because it is preparing for a danger.

We can therefore say that while anxiety is in the future, fear is in the present, because we feel fear when we see a danger in front of us, which makes us instinctively activate our sense of survival.

Sadness and Joy

In third place we have the emotion of sadness, which is one of the emotions most related to sensitivity and originates from a loss or an unfulfilled purpose.

On the opposite side of sadness we find joy, which is only one of the two positive emotions that we feel in a natural and instinctive way. The latter is a state of mind of those who consider their desires satisfied.

We make a distinction between sensation and emotion. The emotion is something that comes from within, while the feeling as the term itself says is something that comes from the five senses. Often the two terms become interchangeable in common language, although the emotion is something much deeper and hinged in our DNA. Emotions then generate feelings, which in turn can generate emotions, usually of a secondary nature.

Surprise, Contempt and Disgust

In fifth place we find another sometimes positive emotion, surprise. It too has been found in all populations (and animals) and is defined as primordial or universal. It originates from an unexpected event and can be followed by fear or joy. Surprise can also be negative as well as positive.

At number six we can list an emotion that I personally did not think was primary: contempt.

It is a feeling and attitude of total lack of esteem, a disdainful rejection of people or things considered lacking in moral or intellectual dignity.

Have you ever felt contempt for someone or something? Surely you have. The interesting thing is that this is also an emotion found in any population and in animals.

Seventh and final primal emotion is disgust. A repulsive type response characterized by a specific facial expression. In fact, when we feel disgust for something we go to express it physically and in a very obvious way.

4

Recognizing emotions

All these primary emotions that I have listed have a physical and visible feedback.

Clearly they can be more or less disguised depending on what is the mode of emotional approach to the problem.

The point is to recognize the primary emotions to empathically approach the other, but also and above all to review them in ourselves.

To an action A corresponds an output B, so we should ask ourselves "I am sad today, what can be the trigger, the thing that activated my sadness?".

In fact, the moment we recognize sadness, we can go and retrieve the reason for it and once identified we can remove it from our lives, or we can go and work on that sadness and test it by questioning it.

This book has a dual purpose. The first is to make you recognize emotions, the second is to make you reflect on the concept that by "recognizing" emotions you will surely be able to go and intervene on the "cause" of this emotion, whether positive or negative.

There is also a third objective, that of recognizing the emotions in the other with the aim of improving tout-court the quality of communication because if we learn to recognize emotions we can act accordingly.

For example, if our girl shows fear and we realize it even if she doesn't verbalize it, we can intervene reassuring her.

The emotions listed are innate emotions found in any population. For this reason they are defined primary, primordial and universal.

Instead, secondary emotions are those that originate from the combination of primary emotions and that develop with the growth of the individual and social interaction.

We must always remember that we are animals that gradually over centuries and millennia have generated an interaction that gave rise to society.

At first in small groups and then in larger and larger groups. The primary group is the family, in which not only primary emotions can dominate, because there are rules within it.

This marks the transition from nature to culture, so from what we would do naturally to what we learn to be in society and survive with others.

In this regard, the whole theory of Freud's Psychoanalysis is based on a concept. Man instinctively must have sex and kill, he is dominated by Eros and Thanatos, a sexual impulse and a death impulse. Society goes to curb these impulses and this generates neurosis, that is, an unnatural blockage of these drives of ours.

We said that secondary emotions originate from the combination of primary ones. I hope that this introductory hat on emotions makes you reflect on what you feel, make you look for emotions in the other and intervene both with you, identifying the problem that generates the negative emotion, and with the other, trying to help the other and trying to be as empathetic as possible.

Empathy means walking in the other's shoes and this generates a deep connection, which can definitely improve the way you communicate and your relationships.

5

Secondary emotions

As we have said, secondary emotions are more complex than primary ones and need more external elements or heterogeneous thoughts to be activated.

Secondary emotions are mostly the result of social impositions and are more articulated, complex and fascinating, because they have different nuances.

We have seen that primary ones are emotions that are born, develop and originate from our DNA and are probably easier to recognize, are immediate and are more instinctual and instinctive.

Instead, the secondary ones are a combination and therefore something more particular to study.

We also note here how the secondary emotions have a predominance of negativity.

Cheerfulness and Envy

This time, however, we start with a positive emotion, joy. It is a different emotion from joy, which we remember defining as the positive state of those who see their desires fulfilled.

We are cheerful when we experience a feeling of full and vivid satisfaction of the soul. You understand how this emotion is more articulated and nuanced.

In second place we cannot but put envy.

This is a very strong emotional state that arises from a comparative process with the other.

In this emotional state, the subject feels a strong desire to have what the other has.

The reasoning behind it is: "He has this, I don't, so I would like to have what he has".

On a social level, envy is quite dominant, especially in modern society, because we no longer have only primary desires or needs.

In modern society, needs have changed a lot.

When we feel envy we have a sense of lack and resentment towards the other, because then envy is also reflected in a negative or aggressive way.

In contemporary society, envy is manifested in a more passive-aggressive way, i.e. by holding back one's frustration and then exploding it with small charges of dynamite, the famous little arrows.

A sort of emotional literacy is, in my opinion, necessary to progress in personal growth and in social terms. Having emotional know-how is something that many people lack, but it is an absolutely important and required soft skill. I've noticed this during my coaching sessions: when I ask for the emotion felt in a certain moment there is always a lot of confusion.

Shame

In third place we put shame.

This is clearly the most social emotional reaction of all, because it is the reaction you feel as a result of transgressing a rule.

In society certain rules are imposed, such as the prohibition of incest. Shame is felt precisely as a reflection of a transgression of one of these imposed rules.

There is a whole series of basic impositions that, if broken, arouse a sense of shame. In this also religion has played and plays a fundamental role.

We need only think of the Original Sin, which generated a profound sense of shame in Adam and Eve. So all our culture, I am talking about

Italy in this case, of Catholic type is based on a sense of shame and modesty.

Shame is a very complex emotion, which cannot be isolated, but it should always be analyzed from a social context point of view.

Anxiety

We have already mentioned the emotion of anxiety as a foreshadowing of danger, future and distant.

We experience nostalgia (which brings us back to the past) and anxiety (which projects us into the future).

The latter derives from the fear not of a concrete danger, but of a hypothetical danger, normally dictated by a past experience.

For example, if someone had a bad skiing accident when he was young, as an adult he will have anxiety about going skiing.

Even if nothing happens, our brain is activated with a function of protection and protection of our safety.

Anxiety serves precisely to protect our bodies and our lives from problems and complexities that have not yet occurred.

Unfortunately, there is a risk that it becomes a loop, a circle, a cat biting its own tail and could become blocking.

The only way to deal with anxiety is to jump into the danger to subconsciously and sub-communicatively understand that there really is no danger.

Gradually, an approach to the problem and an increasingly global awareness can lead to the dissolution of the anxiety. However, I disagree about resolving it quickly, as this is something to do when you feel ready and with the help of a professional.

For example, people have anxiety about exams because probably when they were children the questioning was seen in the form of severity and aroused shame in the case of a negative outcome. So, today exam anxiety stems from a fear related to something that happened in the past and that formed us, because when we are children we are like 'sponges' that absorb and experience emotions in a more exaggerated way.

As children, everything seems bigger to us, even on a materialistic as well as emotional level.

There is therefore the risk that by absorbing certain anxieties and fears as children, they create discomfort in adulthood. We must therefore realize that anxiety is derived from a past trigger and that it is an imaginary projection of a future that normally does not occur.

Resignation

In fifth place is the secondary emotion of resignation.

It is the disposition of mind of those who accept with patience a pain or misfortune.

We feel resigned when we have no more hope, when we realize that we are unable to intervene, when the cartridges are finished and we are at the mercy of other events.

We resign ourselves to something on which we can no longer intervene.

This emotion is very important, as it makes us realize that we cannot have control over everything. One of the evils of modern society is the urge to control, when often and willingly we can not have control over everything and we could never have it and therefore we resign ourselves.

Jealousy

We have another emotional state related to possession: jealousy. An emotional state that stems from the fear of losing something that already belongs to us.

This emotion, more than related to objects, is derived from the fear of losing a person who is dear to us.

This is an emotion that we must pay close attention to, because especially in romantic relationships it stems from an extremely dangerous root: possession.

It is something that we normally have in mind at the level of objects: I own a computer and I am jealous of my computer, so if they touch it or take it away I feel a sense of anger because I have been deprived of it.

It is a different case with people: people are not owned.

It is dangerous to think that a person is our possession or that we are in possession of other people. So, this emotional state that comes from the fear of losing something or someone is dangerous, because then jealousy generates anger and the situation could degenerate.

We should never consider the possibility of owning a person.

People decide to be together, no one is an object and no one is in possession of the other. There has to be some sort of pleasant emotional interchange and growth.

If jealousy intervenes, for whatever reason it happens, it has to be a huge wake-up call that makes you wonder why you are jealous and why you have this tendency to possess (which is not good).

Hope

In point seven we have hope. An emotion that goes hand in hand with resignation and is that tendency that we have to believe that some events or phenomena are manageable and controllable, therefore addressable towards better outcomes.

Hope is a very powerful feeling, but in practice it will never be self-fulfilling. However, it can be an excellent input to begin a series of actions aimed at achieving certain goals.

Hope is an emotion of acquired origin and is something that can give the La to certain actions and therefore convince us to carry them out to reach our goal.

Forgiveness

In the eighth point we find another secondary emotion, forgiveness.

It is the replacement of the negative emotions that follow a perceived offense.

It occurs when we feel anger and fear but replace them with positive emotions, such as empathy and compassion. Forgiveness is fundamentally the basis of the Catholic-Christian religion.

Everyone can make mistakes, maybe we feel anger at first, but then we rationally decide to replace those negative emotions that hurt us and the other person with positive emotions.

It is not always possible to forgive, but basically we have a replacement of a negative emotion with a positive one. It is a very interesting, learned, rational and logical process of choice.

The Offense

In step nine we have what is a moral damage that is done to another person, namely the offense.

When we feel offended, this happens because we feel that something touches our "raw nerves". So, someone touches our moral values and we resent that person and what they have done.

We focus first on what they did and then on the person themselves.

This is the reason why when a story ends and maybe we are left, and therefore we are offended, we identify that person with that extremely negative gesture without thinking about the happy years we thought together.

So, the sense of offence is so powerful that it can cloud many positive things.

Negative emotions, in fact, have a specific weight ten times higher than positive ones. So we often go to give much more weight to negative events and emotions than positive ones.

We can also use this in communication, knowing that with a negative emotion we will have much more powerful reactions than with a positive one.

Nostalgia

Secondary emotion number ten is a state of malaise caused by an acute longing for a distant place, an absent or lost thing or person, or a finished situation that you would like to relive: nostalgia.

It represents a kind of sadness linked to a past event, place or situation that we have a strong desire to relive.

It is said that you can also die of nostalgia: there are also other animal species, such as canaries, in which when the partner dies, the other is left to die.

Remorse

The eleventh secondary emotion is remorse.

A state of disturbance or psychological pain experienced by those who believe they have behaved or acted in a manner contrary to their moral code.

When we talk about morals, we are talking about society. One feels remorse for having done something that should not have been done, something that with the passage of time has proved to be unhelpful, or in any case has generated damage to our person or others.

Remorse can be mild or acute, like all these emotions.

Disappointment

As a secondary emotion we have disappointment.

A state of mind that derives from sadness and caused by the realization that the expectations and hopes that have been cultivated are not matched in reality.

In the moment in which we generate through hope an expectation that is not fulfilled, we feel a sense of disappointment.

We therefore understand how these secondary emotions are much more complex emotions that need many more external elements and heterogeneous thoughts to be activated. By recognizing these emotions in ourselves and others, we are able to get a leg up and connect more authentically and deeply with each other.

When dealing with communication, knowing these processes is critical to being able to communicate your emotions or to elicit them in your interlocutor.

I'm sure many of you knew these emotions, but few of you went into detail and even fewer of you reasoned about what you felt based on certain inputs.

Naming things makes them exist.

If we can figure out that that is remorse rather than disappointment, or longing rather than jealousy, we are in a different league than most people, who are emotionally illiterate. Knowing our emotions guarantees us a higher quality of our lives and relationships with others and, as a result, personal growth toward a better version of ourselves.

6

Where do we feel our emotions?

In this section we will try to interpret what is an emotion map that tells us in which parts of the body certain emotions occur on a physical level, including anger, fear, disgust, happiness, anxiety, depression, worry and pride.

There is a study still being done by some Finnish scientists, who have located what we feel in our bodies based on different emotions.

More than 700 candidates have been analyzed and the result is what in English is called a heat map.

It corresponds to the design of the human body and in the areas where a certain emotion occurs it indicates its intensity with a spot of a warm color. The red color indicates an accumulation of a lot of energy, the yellow color a little less and the lack of warm colors indicates instead the absence of energy, marked by the presence of cold colors, from blue to black.

Let's check if these intuitions correspond to real life.

This is a lesson that will allow you to know yourself better and go to face reactions with more awareness, making you aware of what is happening in your body as a reaction to an external stimulus.

Let's look in detail at what triggers certain emotions in our bodies and where, physically, they occur.

Let's start with a very strong emotion that concentrates all the energy in the upper part of the body, anger.

When we are angry we have in the upper body a time bomb ready to explode.

The lower part of the body remains neutral, except for a small reaction of the feet. In particular, the hands are rich in energy and this can explain why when we lose our temper we have the instinct to vent this energy maybe beating our fists on the table.

Let's move on to the feeling that we have all experienced at least once in our lives: fear.

Fear has a paralyzing force and makes us unable to react.

The thing we can identify as a reaction to fear is inactivity of the legs and arms. The energy is basically determined by adrenaline and is concentrated mainly in the upper part of the body, therefore head, chest and especially at the level of the heart.

In fact, when we are afraid the heartbeat accelerates in a dizzy way and it almost seems as if the heart jumps out of our chest.

Fear is a feeling of animal origin, which has saved us from many situations, just think of the primitive man who had to be afraid to escape from dangerous animals.

So it is something innate and common to everyone.

The energy of fear paralyzes us, we are unable to act and it can be followed by a counter reaction, such as escape for example.

Disgust is another feeling that we have all experienced and that is clearly seen by a great concentration of energy at the level of the throat and abdominal organs.

It is the classic feeling of when we taste something we don't like or find ourselves in a situation that we don't like.

Then we have the most beautiful of emotions, happiness. This is perhaps the most powerful emotion because it can ignite and illuminate every part of the body.

When we are happy, in fact, we radiate joy and energy from all pores, it is an all-encompassing feeling and an irrepressible joy that involves every cell of our body.

On the opposite side we find the feeling of sadness, which turns off the body from any vital energy, but unlike depression is temporary and we always have a "little light" that makes us think that things will get better.

This is thanks to resilience, that is the ability to adapt to new situations by defeating states of sadness caused by exogenous or endogenous conditions.

The important thing is to realize how sadness takes energy away from our body, but maintains a glimmer of hope and energy that makes us think that we will succeed.

Then there is the emotion of surprise. Surprise is something that catches us unexpectedly and wakes us up from the slumber of routine.

When someone gives us a surprise we go from a calm state to one of excitement.

This emotion occurs at the level of the heart and mind, so when we feel surprised in front of an action or a fact, we go to explicate our energy at the level of the chest and head.

This contrapasso from a static situation to a dynamic one gives us the classic sense of surprise, an injection of adrenaline.

On the other hand, when we are apathetic, and therefore feel an emotion of neutrality, we do not feel any particular emotion.

Apathy is in fact the lack of reaction to stimuli and our body expresses this feeling very clearly, in fact within the study the neutral situation is marked by the color blue and black, especially at the level of the lungs and limbs.

There are no energy peaks, we don't have any kind of emotional turning point, but we are passive to what happens outside and inside our body.

A sensation also of animal origin is anxiety, that is the mental anticipation of something that could happen but normally does not.

Normally, this sensation occurs in the thoracic area, as if to identify something that oppresses our chest.

You have undoubtedly experienced this feeling of chest and heart oppression. It leaves you powerless and unable to act. Some people somatize it at the level of the throat, while in this state the limbs remain inactive.

Let's talk about love, the most intense and noble feeling that causes an explosive storm of emotions in the upper part of the body, up to the pelvis and sexual organs, because we are animals and this feeling is related to our goal of reproduction.

Even the abdomen is pervaded by a whirlwind, along with the head, chest and limbs, and this would explain the famous empty stomach with the famous "butterflies".

The interesting thing about this aspect of love, which involves the whole body, is that the part of the legs remains neutral.

Hence the feeling of walking suspended.

Remember that listening to our body is the best way to know ourselves better because the body never lies.

Let's move on to one of the worst sensations a person can experience, depression, which completely annihilates any vital spark, we are completely turned off and the body appears neutral to any stimulus.

There is a sense of apathy and inability to react to external agents. The body does not react to the stimulus and is also cold and immobilized, in a sort of mental hibernation from which it is very difficult to get out.

This is the reason why those suffering from depression can hardly get out of this stasis alone, but need external help. This lack of responsiveness to stimuli differentiates it from sadness, which instead, as mentioned, keeps a small light on.

Contempt is an emotion that for some is expressed in the head while the rest of the body is neutral. In particular, to demonstrate our animal nature, the sensual apparatus shows a greater coldness.

Instead, when we feel pride our chest swells, hence "swollen with pride", and it is a very beautiful sensation that is expressed in the upper part of the body, especially in the head and rib cage.

So we have shame, which is very easy to recognize because it concentrates a great energy at the level of the face and in particular of the cheeks, which explains precisely why we blush.

When we are ashamed, our cheeks are red but the rest of the body is cold. So all the energy goes to accumulate in one portion of the body and it is in fact a very intense sensation.

To conclude, let's talk about envy, a feeling that inflames us at the level of the face and heart, as if to show how it is an emotion that starts almost entirely from our mind.

In fact, at the animal level envy does not exist, it is a social emotion that takes place in the mind and heart.

We have seen this long list of emotions and where in our bodies they go to occur.

I invite you to use these tips to do a self-analysis and try to listen to yourself, so you can communicate better with others but also with yourself.

Listening to what we are feeling in a specific moment is definitely a reason for growth and a way to feel better about ourselves and others.

7

Towards self-realization

It can be interesting to go and face the analysis of our needs, because we have seen the primary and secondary emotions, but in a more holistic, complete and complex vision it is useful to try to understand what the human being really aims at.

A scholar named Maslow created a pyramid of needs with primary needs at the base and more and more secondary needs towards the tip.

The purpose of this pyramid is to explain how we have some unavoidable needs, but through a continuous process towards self-realization we go to meet many others.

It is important to know the needs in order to understand the context within which we are moving and in which a man lives: what are the drives and impulses?

At the base of Maslow's Pyramid we can go to indicate what are needs aimed at survival, which is the first thing that drives us to act by influencing our behavior.

Once survival is assured, we can move to the higher step of Maslow's Pyramid, and so on up to the top.

In the top rung we find self-actualization, so the fullness of a complete and satisfying life.

In Maslow's Pyramid we have five levels. In the lowest level there is the physiology, the primary needs, that is all those needs that serve to ensure survival (oxygen, food, water, sleep …) that are often summarized in the term "homeostasis", or the natural tendency to achieve a relative physiological stability.

The second level is constituted by the needs that, if satisfied, guarantee our security (health, well-being, family protection, financial security…). In a "typical" contemporary society, we can place physical, employment, moral, family, health and property security on this step.

We note that as the pyramid is scaled up, needs become increasingly social and less physiological.

In the third step we find the needs of belonging (friendship, family affection, sexual intimacy) and is a level that includes love relationships, social groups, the Church, religious organizations and so on.

Feeling belonging to a group is very important for us human beings. To avoid problems such as loneliness, anxiety and depression it is important to feel loved, appreciated and accepted.

At the fourth step we have the need for esteem, that is the search for assurance of who we are and what we are worth within the social fabric.

So we find the need for mutual respect, personal fulfillment, self-control, self-esteem.

Esteem comes from the need to feel appreciated and respected.

We need to make sense of our value and this sense is also dictated by what others think of us.

It can be said that the third and fourth levels of Maslow's Pyramid represent the psychological needs that if satisfied guarantee personal well-being.

Finally, at the tip of the Pyramid we find self-realization (morality, creativity, spontaneity, problem solving, acceptance, absence of prejudices).

This is a state of well-being in which the human being goes to realize himself in all his glory.

Maslow said that this level of self-actualization is what a human being can be and should be, hence the highest human fulfillment.

In Maslow's words, "Self-actualization could be described as the full use or exploitation of one's talents, abilities, and potentialities. People who are able to self-actualize seem to be satisfied in that they are giving the best of what they are capable of. They are individuals who have developed or are developing to their fullest potential."

So the moment we live a full life, have a satisfying job and family, are able to express our creativity and find it easy to satisfy our impulses, even psychological ones, we arrive at self-actualization. This can take a lifetime.

I told you about this Maslow Pyramid to make you understand that we, even if we do not realize it, respond daily to some innate needs, archetypal and common to all.

Failure to meet these goals and needs can generate emotions.

For example, if we do not self-actualize we will be sad, if we follow badly some steps we may feel nostalgia, anger or confusion.

So, emotions are the direct result of our satisfaction or dissatisfaction of basic needs. If at the level of belonging we do not feel appreciated and do not belong to anything, we will feel a sense of sadness, if we lose this belonging we will feel nostalgia.

8

Conclusions

It is therefore important to be able to understand the importance of following a pattern in one's life, to understand if one is fulfilling needs and the emotions that arise from them, as well as the negative emotions that arise from the dissatisfaction of the needs listed in the Pyramid.

So, starting from the bottom, from the more physiological ones to the more psychological ones of self-realization.

Physiological needs, such as breathing, nutrition, sex, sleep, also known as homeostasis; security needs, such as physical security, employment, economic security, moral security, family security, health, property.

In the next two levels we find the psychological needs: those of belonging, feeling appreciated within a social context in which we share some values and to which we belong; those of esteem and therefore self-control, self-realization, respect, self-esteem. In the final part we find self-realization which is what man should aspire to.

This is a difficult and complex subject, which often requires a lot of time to be internalized. But I can guarantee you that the moment you know the pattern on which we move, you will be able to take the right path without going haphazardly.

You cannot live your life blindfolded, you must recognize in a deep system of self-analysis what is the designated path, that is, your needs and emotions.

The moment we know and recognize them, an exponential growth of our value and our power to control our life can take place.

I am Emanuele, I am a teacher of emotional communication, storytelling and creativity. I was very happy to create this book for you and I hope it will help you to grow on a personal level, to better recognize the emotions in yourself and in others and to understand that at the base of personal evolution there is a pattern common to all, which should serve as a mirror to understand what stage of our lives we are in.

Note: apart from physiological needs, needs do not necessarily have to be followed in this order. There may be those who value belonging over esteem, or those who are not interested in psychological needs and focus only on primary physiological and safety needs.

In order to reach your full potential, keep in mind that this diagram can be very helpful in asking yourself, "Am I meeting my needs? Are my emotions suggesting that to some extent they have not been fulfilled?".

Only by knowing this theory will you be able to identify them and take action. In life you must identify critical issues and then act on them, otherwise you will get nowhere.

Training and Coaching

If you are interested in starting a training program with me, visit https://www.emozionare.net. You will be able to book a free, no obligation phone consultation.

My Books

Find a list of all my books on Amazon by searching for the keyword 'Emanuele M. Barboni Dalla Costa' or by clicking on this link.

Free Podcast (Italian)

I publish my weekly communication and creative lessons at https://anchor.fm/podcastemozionale

www.ingramcontent.com/pod-product-compliance
Lightning Source LLC
Chambersburg PA
CBHW051131250726
48655CB00007B/2996